MONOLOGUES

FROM

OSCAR WILDE

edited by

Ian Michaels

CONTENTS

WOMEN

Salome. 1893.

In this scene, Salome reveals her passion for Iokanaan (John the Baptist), and although rebuffed by him, continues to lust after him.

SALOME

Thy body is hideous. It is likely the body of a leper. It is like a plastered wall, where vipers have crawled; like a plastered wall where the scorpions have made their nest. It is like a whited sepulchre, full of loathsome things. It is horrible, thy body is horrible. It is of thy hair that I am enamoured, Iokanaan. Thy hair is like clusters of grapes, like the clusters of black grapes that hang from the vine-trees of Edom in the land of the Edomites. They hair is like the cedars of Lebanon, like the great cedars of Lebanon that give their shade to the lions and the robbers who would hide them by day. The long black nights, when the moon hides her face, when the stars are afraid, are not so black as thy hair . . . Suffer me to touch thy hair.

Thy hair is horrible. It is covered with mire and dust. It is like a crown of thorns placed on thy head. It is like a knot of serpents coiled round thy neck. I love not thy hair . . . It is thy mouth that I desire, Iokanaan. Thy mouth is like a band of scarlet on a tower of ivory. It is like a pomegranate cut in twain with a knife of ivory. The pomegranate flowers that blossom in the gardens of Tyre, and are redder than roses, are not so red. The red blasts of trumpets that hearld the approach of kings, and make afraid the enemy, are not so red. Thy mouth is redder then the feet of those who tread the wine in the wine-press. It is redder than the feet of the doves who inhabit the temples and are fed by the priests. It is redder than the feet of him who cometh from a forest where he hath slain a lion, and seen gilded tigers. Thy mouth is like a branch of coral that they keep for the kings! . . . It is like the vermilion that the Moabites find in the mines of Moab, the vermilion that the kings take from them. It is like the bow of the King of the Persians, that is painted with vermilion, and is tipped with coral. There is nothing in the world so red as thy mouth . . . Suffer me to kiss thy mouth.

Salome.   1893.

*After her dance of the seven veils, Salome is rewarded with the
head of Iokanaan (John the Baptist). She begins making love to
the head, and is ordered killed by Herod following this scene.*

SALOME

(She leans over the cistern and listens.) There is no
sound. I hear nothing. Why does not he cry out, this
man? Ah! if any man sought to kill me, I would cry
out, I would struggle, I would not suffer . . . Strike,
strike, Naaman, strike, I tell you . . . No, I hear
nothing. There is silence, a terrible silence. Ah!
something has fallen upon the ground. I heard
something fall. It is the sword of the executioner. He is
afraid, this slave. He has dropped his sword. He dares
not kill. He is a coward, this slave! Let soldiers be
sent. *(She sees the Page of Herodias and addresses
him.)* Come hither. Thou wert the friend of him who
is dead, wert thou not? Well, I tell thee, there are not
dead men enough. Go to the soldiers and bid them go
down and bring me the thing I ask, the thing that the
Tetrarch has promised me, the thing that is mine. *(The
Page recoils. She turns to the soldiers.)* Hither, ye
soldiers. Get thee down into this cistern and bring me
the head of this man. Tetrarch, Tetrarch, command
your soldiers that they bring me the head of Iokanaan.
Well! I will kiss it now. I will bite it with my teeth as
one bites a ripe fruit. Yes, I will Kiss they mouth,
Iokanaan. I said it; did I not say it? I said it. Ah! I will
kiss it now . . . But wherefore dost thou not look at me,
Iokanaan? Thine eyes that were so terrible, so full of

3

rage and scorn, are shut now. Wherefore are they shut? Open thine eyes! Lift up thine eyelids, Iokanaan! Wherefore does thou not look at me? Art thou afraid of me, Iokanaan, that thou wilt not look at me? . . . And thy tongue, that was like a red snake darting poison, it moves no more, it speaks no words, Iokanaan, that scarlet viper that spat its venom upon me. It is strange, is it not? How it is that the red viper stirs no longer? . . . Thou wouldst have none of me, Iokanaan. Thou rejectedst me. Thou dist speak evil words against me. Thou dist bear thyself toward me as to a harlot, as to a woman who is a wanton, to me, Salome, daughter of Herodias, Princess of Judaea! Well, I still live, but thou art dead, and thy head belongs to me. I can do with it what I will. I can throw it to the dogs and to the birds of the air. That which the dogs leave, the birds of the air shall devour . . .Ah, Iokanaan, Iokanaan, thou wert the man I loved alone among men! All other men were hateful to me. But thou wert beautiful! Thy body was a column of ivory set upon feet of silver. It was a garden full of doves and lilies of silver. It was a tower of silver decked with shields of ivory. There was nothing in the world so white as thy body. There was nothing in the world so black as thy hair. In the world there was nothing so red as thy mouth. Thy voice was a censer that scattered strange perfumes, and when I looked on thee I heard a strange music. Ah! wherefore dist thou not look at me, Iokanaan? With the cloak of thine hands, and with the cloak of thy blasphemies thou dist hide thy face. Thou dist put upon thine eyes the covering of him who would see his God. Well, thou hast seen thy God, Iokanaan, but me, me, thou dist never see. If thou hadst seen me thou hadst loved me. I

4

saw thee, and I loved thee. Oh, how I loved thee . . . I am athirst for thy beauty; I am hungry for thy body; and neither wine nor apples can appease my desire. What shall I do now, Iokanaan? Neither the floods nor the great waters can quench my passion. I was a princess, and thou dist scorn me. I was a virgin and thou dist take my virginity from me. I was chaste, and thou dist fill my veins with fire . . . Ah! ah! wherefore didst thou not look at me? If thou hadst looked at me thou hadst loved me. Well I know that thou wouldst have loved me, and the mystery of Love is greater than the mystery of Death.

The Importance Of Being Earnest. 1895. Act III.

Lady Bracknell refuses to allow Jack to marry Gwendolen.

LADY BRACKNELL

Come here. Sit down. Sit down immediately. Hesitation of any kind is a sign of mental decay in the young, of physical weakness in the old. Apprised, sir, of my daughter's sudden flight by her trusty maid, whose confidence I purchased by means of a small coin, I followed her at once by a luggage train. Her unhappy father is, I am glad to say, under the impression that she is attending a more than usually lengthy lecture at the University Extension Scheme on the Influence of a Permanent Income on Thought. I do not propose to undeceive him. Indeed, I have never undeceived him on any question. I would consider it wrong. But of course, you will clearly understand that all the communication between yourself and my daughter must cease immediately from this moment. On this point, as indeed all points, I am firm. I do not know whether there is anything peculiarly exciting in the air of this particular part of Hertfordshire, but the number of engagements that go on seems to me considerably above the proper average that statistics have laid down for our guidance. I think some preliminary inquiry on my part would not be out of place. Mr. Worthing, is Miss Cardew at all connected with any of the larger railway stations in London? I merely desire information.

The Importance Of Being Earnest. 1895. Act III.

The superficiality of Lady Bracknell is emphasized in this scene.

LADY BRACKNELL

(Sitting down again.) A moment, Mr. Worthing. A hundred and thirty pounds! And in Funds! Miss Cardew seems to me a most attractive young lady, now that I look at her. Few girls of the present day have any real solid qualities, any of the qualities that last, and improve with time. We live, I regret to say, in an age of surfaces. *(To Cecily.)* Come over here, dear. Pretty child! Your dress is sadly simple, and your hair seems almost as Nature might have left it. But we can soon alter that. A thoroughly experienced French maid produces a really marvellous result in a very brief space of time. I remember recommending one to young Lady Lancing, and after three months her own husband did not know her. Kindly turn round, sweet child. *(She turns.)* No, the side view is what I want. *(Cecily presents her profile.)* Yes, quiet as I expected. There are distinct social possibilities in your profile. The two weak points in our age are its want of principle and its want of profile. The chin a little higher, dear. Style largely depends on the way the chin is worn. They are worn very high at present. *(Algernon grunts with disgust.)* Algernon! Never speak disrespectfully of society, Algernon. Only people who can't get into it do that.

A Woman Of No Importance. 1893. Act IV.

In this monologue, Mrs. Arbuthnot explains to her son, Gerald, why she will not marry his father, Lord Illingworth.

MRS. ARBUTHNOT

Men don't understand what mothers are. I am no different from other women except in the wrong done me and the wrong I did, and my very heavy punishments and great disgrace. And yet, to bear you I had to look on death. To nurture you I had to wrestle with it. Death fought with me for you. All women have to fight with death to keep their children. Death, being childless, wants our children from us. Gerald, when you were naked I clothed you, when you were hungry I gave you food. Night and day all that long winter I tended you. No office is too mean, no care to lowly for the thing we women love - and oh! how I loved you. Not Hannah Samuel more. And you needed love, for you were weakly, and only love could have kept you alive. Only love can keep anyone alive. And boys are careless often and without thinking give pain, and we always fancy that when they come to a man's estate and know us better, they will repay us. But it is not so. The world draws them from our side, and they make friends with whom they are happier than they are with us, and have amusements from which we are barred, and interests that are not ours; and they are unjust to us often, for when they find life bitter they blame us for it, and when they find it sweet we do not taste its sweetness with them . . . You made many friends and went into their houses and were glad with them, and I, knowing my secret, did not dare to follow, but stayed home and closed the door, shut out the sun and sat in the darkness. What should I have done in honest households? My past was ever with me . . . And you thought I didn't care for the pleasant things in life. I tell you I longed for them, but did not dare to touch them, feeling I had no right. You thought I was happier working amongst the poor. That was my mission, you imagined. It was not, but where else was I to go? The sick do not ask if the hand that smooths their pillow is pure, nor the dying care if the lips that touch their brow have known the kiss of sin. It was you I thought of all the time; I gave to them the love you did not need: lavished on them a love that was not theirs . . . And you thought I spend too much of my time going to Church, and in Church duties. But where else could I turn? God's house is the only house where sinners are made welcome, and you were always in my heart, Gerald, too much in my heart. For, though day after day, at morn or evensong, I have knelt in God's house, I have never repented to my sin. How could I repent of my sin when you, my love, were its fruit? Even now that you are bitter to me I cannot repent. I do not. You are more to me than innocence. I would rather be your mother - oh! much rather! - then have been always pure . . . Oh, don't you see? don't you understand? It is my dishonour that has made you so dear to me. It is my disgrace that has bound you so closely to me. It is the price I paid for you - the price of soul and body - that makes me love you as I do. Oh, don't ask me to do this horrible thing. Child of my shame, be still the child of my shame!

An Ideal Husband. 1895. Act II.

Mabel Chiltern, Sir Robert Chiltern's sister, has been proposed to by Sir Robert's secretary, Tommy Trafford.

MABEL CHILTERN

Well, Tommy has proposed to me again. Tommy really does nothing but propose to me. He proposed to me last night in the music-room, when I was quite unprotected, as there was an elaborate trio going on. I din't dare make the smallest repartee, I need hardly tell you. If I had it would have stopped the music at once. Musical people are so absurdly unreasonable. They always want one to perfectly dumb at the very moment when one is longing to be absolutely deaf. Then he proposed to me in broad daylight this morning, in front of that dreadful statue of Achillies. Really, the things that go on in front of that work of art are quite appalling. The police should interfere. At luncheon I saw by the glare in his eyes that he was going to propose again, and I just managed to check him in time by assuring him that I was a bimetallist. Fortunately I don't know what bimetallism means. And I don't believe anybody else does either. But the observation crushed Tommy for ten minutes. He looked quite shocked. And then Tommy is so annoying in the way he purposes. If he proposed at the top of his voice, I should not mind so much. That might produce some effect on the public. But he does it in a horrible confidential way. When Tommy wants to be romantic he talks to one just like a doctor.

Lady Windermere's Fan. 1892. Act I.

The Dutchess of Berwick reveals to her daughter Agatha and to Lady Windermere her belief that Lord Windermere is having an affair with Mrs. Erlynne.

DUTCHESS OF BERWICK

Don't you really know? I assure you we're all distressed about it. Only last night at dear Lady Jansen's every one was saying how extraordinary it was that, of all men in London, Windermere should behave in such a way.

He goes to see here continually, and stops for hours at a time, and while he is there she is not a home to anyone. Not that many ladies call on her, dear, but she has a great many disreputable men friends - my own brother particularly, as I told you - and that is what makes it so dreadful about Windermere. We looked upon him as being such a model husband, but I' m afraid there is no doubt about it. My dear nieces - you know the Saville girls, don't you? - such nice domestic creatures - plain, dreadfully plain, but so good - well, they're always at the window doing fancy work, and making ugly things for the poor, which I think so useful of them in these dreadful socialistic days, and this terrible woman has taken a house in Curzon Street, right opposite them - such a respectable street, too! I don't know what we're coming to! And they tell me Windermere goes there four and five times a week - they see him. They can't help it - and although they never talk scandal, they - well, of course - they remark on it to everyone. And the worst of it all is that I have been told that this woman has got a great deal of money out of somebody, for it seems that she came to London six months ago without anything at all to speak of, and now she has this charming house in Mayfair, drives her ponies in the Park every afternoon and all - well, all - since she has known poor Windermere. The whole of London knows it. That is why I felt it was better to come and talk to you, and advise you to take Windermere away at once to Homburg or to Aix, where he'll have something to amuse him, and where you can watch him all day long. I assure you, my dear, that on several occasions after I was first married, I had to pretend to be very ill, and was obliged to drink the most unpleasant waters, merely to get Berwick out of town.. He was so extremely susceptible. Though I am bound to say he never gave away any large sums of money to anybody. He is far to high-principled for that!

Lady Windermere's Fan. 1892. Act III.

Lady Windermere, believing that her husband is cheating on her, goes to the rooms of Lord Darlington, an aristocratic bachelor who is infatuated with her.

LADY WINDERMERE

(Standing by the fireplace. Betraying the convulsive nervous distress of the conventional lady in the most unconventional place for Victorian ladies: bachelor chambers at a late hour. During the following soliloquy she paces about impatiently, fear and fretfulness alternating with irresolution and indecision.) Why doesn't he come? This waiting is horrible. He should be here. Why is he not here, to wake by passionate words some fire within me? I am cold - cold as a loveless thing. Arthur must have read my letter by this time. If he cared for me, he would have come after me, would have taken me back by force. But he doesn't care. He's entrammeled by this woman - fascinated by her - dominated by her. If a woman wants to hold a man she has merely to appeal to what is worst in him. We make gods of men and they leave us. Others make brutes of them and they fawn and are faithful. How hideous life is! . . . Oh! it was mad of me to come here, horribly mad. And yet which is the worst. I wonder, to be at the mercy of a man who loves one, or the wife of a man who in one's own house dishonors one? What woman knows? What woman in the whole world? But will he love me always, this man to whom I am giving my life? What do I bring to him? Lips that have lost the note of joy, eyes that are blighted

13

by tears, chill hands and icy heart. I bring him nothing. I must go back - no; I can't go back, my letter has put me in their power - Arthur would not take me back! That fatal letter! No! Lord Darlington leaves England tomorrow. I will go with him - I have no choice. *(Sits down for a few moments. Then starts up and puts on her cloak.)* No, no! I will go back, let Arthur do with me what he pleases. I can't wait here. It has been madness my coming. I must go at once. As for Lord Darlington - Oh! here he is! What shall I do? What can I say to him? Will he let me go away at all? I have heard that men are brutal, horrible . . . Oh! *(She hides her face in her hands.)*

Lady Windermere's Fan. 1892. Act IV.

*After being discovered in Lord Darlington's room by Mrs.
Erlynne, Lady Windermere is sure that Mrs. Erlynne will reveal
all to Lord Windermere.*

LADY WINDERMERE

She is sure to tell him. I can fancy a person doing a
wonderful act of self-sacrifice, doing it spontaneously,
recklessly, nobly - and afterwards finding out that it
costs too much. Why should she hesitate between her
ruin and mine? . . . How strange! I would have publicly
disgraced her in my own house. She accepts public
disgrace in the house of another to save me . . . There is
bitter irony in things, a bitter irony in the way we talk
of good and bad women . . . Oh, what a lesson! And
what a pity that in life we only get our lessons when
they are of no use to us! For even if she doesn't tell, I
must. Oh, the shame of it, the shame of it. To tell it is
to live it all again. Actions are the first tragedy in life,
words are the second. Words are perhaps the worst.
Words a merciless . . . I don't think now that people can
be divided into the good and the bad as though they
were two separate races of creations. What are called
good women may have terrible things in them, mad
moods of recklessness, assertion, jealousy, sin. Bad
women, as they are termed, may have in them sorrow,
repentance, pity, sacrifice. And I don't think Mrs.
Erlynne a bad woman - I know she's not.

Lady Windermere's Fan. 1892. Act IV.

Mrs. Erlynne assures Lady Windermere that she need not consider her a threat to her marriage.

MRS. ERLYNNE

Believe what you choose about me. I am not worth a moment's sorrow. But don't spoil your beautiful young life on my account! You don't know what may be in store for you, unless you leave this house at once. You don't know what it is to fall into the pit, to be despised, mocked, abandoned, sneered at - to be an outcast! To find the door shut against one, to have to creep in by hideous byways, afraid every moment lest the mask should be stripped from one's face, and all the while to hear laughter, the horrible laughter of the world, a thing more tragic than all the tears the world has ever shed. You don't know what it is. One pays for one's sin, and then one pays again, and all one's life one pays. You must never know that. - As for me, if suffering be an expiation, then at this moment I have expiated all my faults, whatever they have been; for tonight you have made a heart in one who had it not, made it and broken it. But let that pass. I may have wrecked my own life, but I will not let you wreck yours. You - why you are a mere girl. You haven't got the kind of brains that enables a woman to get back. You have neither the wit nor the courage. You couldn't stand dishonour! No! Go back, Lady Windermere, to the husband who loves you, whom you love. You have a child, Lady Windermere. Go back to that child who even now, in pain or joy, may be calling to you. God gave you that child. He will require from you that you make his life fine, that you watch over him. What answer will you make to God if his life is ruined through you? Back to your house. Lady Windermere - your husband loves you! He has never swerved for a moment from the love he bears you. But even if he had a thousand loves, you must stay with your child. If he was harsh to you, you must stay with your child. If he abandoned you, your place is with your child.

The Dutchess Of Padua. 1883. Act II.

Beatrice, after being chastised by the Duke, and informed as to her station in life, vows to kill herself that evening.

BEATRICE

The stars do fight against me, that is the sum of all. Wherefore will I this night, when my lord is asleep, make good use of my dagger and so end my days. My heart is like a stone that nothing scores save the dagger's edge. There let it find the name that lies hid within. Tonight must death sever me from the Duke, - but yet he too, the old Duke, may die today. Why not? Yesterday his hand was stricken palsied; men have oft been slain by such a stroke, - and why not he? Are there not fever too and ague and fit, as mostly such accompany old age? Nay, nay, he dies not, he is too sinful. The honour-worthy die before their time. The good die, - beside whom, in the hideous pollution of his life, he is a leper. Women and children die; the Duke dies not, he is to sinful.

Can it be, that sin hath a sort of immortality, unknown to virtue? Can it be that the bad man thrives on what to other mortals is death, like poisonous herbs that live from corruption? Nay, nay, God would never suffer that. Yet my lord dies not, he is too sinful. Wherefore 'tis I alone will die tonight. Grim death must so my bridegroom be, the grave my secret pleasure house of joy. A churchyard is the world, and like a coffin, each one doth carry a skeleton within.

18

The Dutchess Of Padua. 1883. Act II.

After refusing to hear the peasants' petition for monetary aid, the Duke of Padua leaves his wife, Beatrice (who was on the side of the peasants). She ponders her unhappy lot in life, feeling that there is no relief in sight. She ponders her unhappy lot in life, the lot of women in general.

BEATRICE

Strange that anyone, blameless to all seeming, doth love the Duke, hangs on his lips, that foully poison every word, and shrinks not from him, as though bound to his service! Well, what of it? it doth concern me not. I stand alone, to love inaccessible. The Duke saith well, I am alone, forlorn and disgraced and belittled - did ever woman stand so all alone as I? The wooer calls us pretty children, saith we be not fit to make a life for ourselves, and therefore doth ruin the life we had. What said I, "Wooers?" We are their goods and chattels, their slaves; we are not so fondly fondled as the dog that licks their hand, and the falcon on their wrist. I said, "Wooers?" Nay, we be bought and sold, our very body is so much pelf to them. I wis it is poor woman's usual lot, - her life, mated with a man she loves not, makes shipwreck on his selfishness; but being usual, 'tis no less hard to bear.Meseems I never yet heard a woman laugh, laugh out of pure light-heartedness, - except one that stood at night i' the public street - poor soul! She had painted lips, a mask of joy to hide her sorrow, and she laughed, pray God I may never laugh so. To die were better! *(She throws herself down before a figure of the Madonna.)* Oh Holy Mary, with the sweet, wan look, ringed with little angel heads that hover round thee, know'st thou no succour fo me?   Oh Mother of God, know'st no succour?

The Dutchess Of Paua. 1883. Act III.

After killing her husband, the Duke, Beatrice justifies her actions to Guido.

BEATRICE

Ah, well for me, had I never seen thee! But bethink thee, 'twas for thee I did it. *(Guido shrinks. She kneels and seizes his hands.)* Nay, Guido, grant me a hearing for a brief space! Till thou camest to Padua, I lived indeed a lamentable life there, but free from thoughts of murder, - subject to the cruelty of my husband, obedient to his unrighteous wishes, as pure as any maid of noble lineage, that now would draw back shuddering from my touch. Then thou camest, Guido, and I heard from thy lips the first words of kindness I had ever listened to since I left France. What then! Thou camest hither, in thine ardent eyes I read the meaning of love, every word from thee rang like music in my numbed soul. Thou dist shine splendid, like the good Saint Michael in Santa Croce, the Church I used to pray in. Shall I ever go there to pray again? In thy bright, young face glowed the clear light of morning - and I loved thee, yet hid my love from thee. Thou didst pay court to me, didst kneel before me, as now I kneel at thy feet. With sweet-sounding oaths thou didst vow love to me, and I trusted thee. I thought how many woman in the world, if they were wedded to this

21

monster, fettered to him, like galley-slaves to a leper, -
that many women would have assailed thee as
temptresses. I did not see. I know, and I had done it,
albeit I had not lain in the very dust before thee, thou
wouldst have loved me unchangingly. *(Timidly after a
pause.)* Whether thou dost understand me even now, I
cannot tell, Guido; for thee I have committed the
outrage, that hath chilled my young blood to ice, for
thee, and thee alone. *(Stretching out her arms.)* Will
thou not speak to me? Love me a little; ah, my youth
hath so lacked love, so yearned for friendship.

The Dutchess Of Padua. 1883. Act III.

*After killing her husband, the Duke, Beatrice begins to feel
remorse and guilt for her deed and begins to descend into
madness. She desires to reverse her actions when she realizes
that she now disgusts Guido.*

BEATRICE

Ah, would to God I could awake the dead, give back to
glassy eye its power of vision, the tongue its erstwhile
flow of words, the heart its life-pulse - but it cannot be.
What's done is done; once dead, dead for aye; no more
the fire warms, or the winter chills with all its snows.
Something is flown; call him, no answer comes, - make
jest, he laughs no more, - stab him, he never bleeds.

Would that I could awake him! Oh God, turn back thy
sun a brief while, erase this night in the book of time
and blot it out. Reverse the sun and let me be what an
hour agone I was. Nay, nay, time stands not still for
anything, the sun stays not his course, though remorse
cry e'er so hoarsely. But thou, beloved, hast no word
of pity more for me? Oh Guido, Guido, kiss me once
again! A woman waxes mad, when so entreated. Wilt
thou not kiss me yet once more?

MEN

Vera; or, The Nihilists. 1881. Act II.

Ivan the Czar has come to the realization that his rule is really in peril, and that he is unable to trust any of his subjects.

CZAR

Vera, the Nihilist, in Moscow! Oh God, were it not better to die at once the dog's death they plot for me than to live as I live now! Never to sleep, or, if I do, to dream such horrid dreams that Hell itself were peace when matched with them. To trust none but those I have bought, to buy none worth trusting! To see a traitor in every smile, poison in ever dish, a dagger in every hand! To lie awake at night, listening from hour to hour for the stealthy creeping of the murderer, for the laying of the damned mine! You are all spies! you are all spies! You worst of all - you, my own son! Which of you is it who hides these bloody proclamations under my pillow, or at the table where I sit? Which of ye all is the Judas who betrays me? The people! The people! A tiger which I have let loose upon myself; but I will fight with it to the death. I am done with half measures. I shall crush these Nihilists at a blow. There shall not be a man of them, ay, or a woman either, left alive in Russia. Am I the Emperor for nothing, that a woman should hold me at bay? Vera Sabouroff shall be in my power, I swear it, before a week is ended, though I burn my whole city to find her.

Vera; or, The Nihilists. 1881. Act II.

Ivan the Czar declares war on the nihilists who are threatening revolution.

CZAR

For two years her hands have been clutching at my throat; for two years she has made my life hell; but I shall have revenge. Martial law, Prince, martial law over the whole Empire; that will give me revenge., A good measure, Prince, eh? a good measure.

(Standing.) I am sick of being afraid. I have done with terror now. From this day I proclaim war against the people - war to their annihilation. As they have dealt with me, so shall I deal with them. I shall grind them to powder, and strew their dust upon the air. There shall be a spy in every man's house, a traitor on every hearth, a hangman in every village, a gibbet in every square. Plague, leprosy, or fever shall be less deadly than my wrath; I will make every frontier a graveyard, every province a lazar-house, and cure the sick by the sword. I shall have peace in Russia, though it be the peace of the dead. Who said I was coward? Who said I was afraid? See, thus shall I crush this people beneath my feet? *(Takes a sword from the table and tramples it.)*

The Importance Of Being Earnest. 1895. Act III.

Jack refuses to give his permission to his ward, Cecily Cardew, to marry Algernon. In this speech, he explains his reasons for his decision.

JACK

I beg your pardon for interrupting you, Lady Bracknell, but this engagement is quite out of the question. I am Miss Cardew's guardian, and she cannot marry without my consent until she comes of age. That consent I absolutely decline to give.It pains me very much to have to speak frankly to you, Lady Bracknell, about your nephew, but the fact is that I do not approve at all os his moral character. I suspect him of being untruthfull.I fear there can be no possible doubt about the matter. This afternoon during my temporary absence in London on an important question of romance, he obtained admission to my house by means of the false pretence of being my brother. Under an assumed name he drank, I've just been informed by my butler, an entire pint bottle of my Perrier-Jouet, Brut '89, a wine I was specially reserving for myself. Continuing his disgraceful deception, he succeeded in the course of the afternoon in alienating the affections of my only ward. He subsequently stayed to tea, and devoured every single muffin. And what makes his conduct all the more heartless is that he was perfectly aware from the first that I have no brother, that I never had a brother, and that I don't intend to have a brother.

The Importance Of Being Earnest. 1895. Act IV.

In attempting to stop the marriage of Algernon to his ward, Cecily Cardew, John Worthing attempts to humiliate Algernon before Lady Brancaster, unaware that Algernon is actually his brother.

JACK

I had hoped, Algernon, to have spared you the necessity of making that painful confession. In the eyes of any sensible person, it puts your conduct in a light that is, if possible, still more disgraceful. As, however, you have chosen yourself to make the matter public, you must bear the necessary consequences. Your nephew, Lady Brancaster, as he has just admitted himself, compelled me at two o'clock this afternoon to pay my own bills, a thing I have not done for years, a thing that is strictly against my principles, a thing that I in every way disapprove of. In taking that attitude, I am not merely speaking for myself, but for others. More young men are ruined now-a-days by paying their bills than by anything else. I know many fashionable young men in London, young men of rank and position, whose rooms are absolutely littered with receipts, and who, with a callousness that seems to me absolutely cynical, have no hesitation in paying ready money for the mere luxuries of life. Such conduct seems to me to strike at the very foundation of things. The only basis for good society is unlimited credit. Without that, Society, as we call it, crumbles. Why is it that we all despise the middle classes? Simply because the pay what they owe.

Lady Windermere's Fan. 1892. Act II.

Lord Darlington reveals his love to Lady Windermere.

LORD DARLINGTON

If I know you at all, I know that you can't live with a
man who treats you like this! What short of life would
you have with him? You would feel that he was lying
to you every moment of the day. You would feel that
the look in his eyes was false, his voice false, his touch
false, his passion false. He would come to you when he
was weary of others; you would have to comfort him.
He would come to you when he was devoted to others;
you would have to charm him. You would have to be
to him the mask of his real life, the cloak to hide his
secret.

Between men and women there is no friendship
possible. There is passion, enmity, worship, love, but
no friendship. I love you -

Yes, I love you! You are more to me than anything in
the whole world. What does your husband give you?
Nothing. Whatever is in him he gives to this wretched
woman, whom he has thrust into your society, into
your home, to shame you before everyone. I offer you
my life -

My life - my whole life. Take it, do with it what you
will . . . I love you - love you as I have never loved any
living thing. From the moment I met you I loved you,
loved you blindly, adoringly, madly! You did not

know it then - you know it now! Leave this house tonight. I won't tell you that the world matters nothing, or the world's voice, or the voice of society. They matter a great deal. They matter far too much. But there are moments when one has to choose between living one's own life, full, entirely, completely - or dragging out some false, shallow, degrading existence that the world in its hypocrisy demands. You have that moment now. Choose! Oh, my love, choose! You have the courage.

There may be six months of pain, of disgrace even, but when you no longer bear his name, when you bear mine, all will be well. Margaret, my love, my wife that shall be some day - yes, my wife! You know it! What are you now? This woman has the place that belongs by right to you. Oh, go - go out of this house, with head erect, with a smile upon your lips, with courage in your eyes. All London will know why you did it; and who will blame you? No One. If they do, what matter? Wrong? What is wrong? It's wrong for a man to abandon his wife for a shameless woman. It is wrong for a wife to remain with a man who so dishonors her. You said once you would make no compromise with things. Make none now. Be brave! Be yourself!

Salome. 1893.

In his passion for his stepdaughter, Salome, Herod agrees to her demands for the head of John the Baptist if she will dance for him.

HEROD

Thou wilt be passing fair for a queen, Salome, if it please thee to ask for half of my kingdom. Will she not be fair as a queen? Ah! it is cold here! There is an icy wind, and I hear . . . wherefore do I hear in the air this beating of wings? Ah! one might fancy a huge black bird that hovers over the terrace. Why can I not see it, this bird? The beat of its wings is terrible. The breath of the wind of its wings is terrible. It is a chill wind. Nay, but it is not cold, it is hot. I am choking. Pour water on my hands. Give me snow to eat. Loosen my mantle. Quick! quick! loosen my mantle. Nay, but leave it. It is my garland that hurts me, my garland of roses. The flowers are like fire. They have burned my forehead. *(He tears the wreath from his head, and throws it to the table.)* Ah! I can breathe now. How red rose petals are! They are like stains of blood on the cloth. That does not matter. It is not wise to find symbols in everything that one sees. It makes life too full of terrors. It were better to say that the stains of blood are as lovely as rose petals. It were better far to say that . . . But we will not speak of this. Now I am happy. I am passing happy. Have I not the right to be happy? Your daughter is going to dance for me. Wilt thou not dance for me, Salome? Thou has promised to dance for me.

Salome. 1893.

Herod attempts to talk Salome out of her demands for the head of John the Baptist.

HEROD

Silence! Do not speak to me . . . Look here, Salome, be sensible. We must be sensible, you know. I have never been harsh with you. I have always loved you . . . Perhaps I have loved you to much. So do not ask that of me. That request is horrible, frightful. I cannot believe you mean it seriously. A man's decapitated head is an ugly thing, do you not realize? Not a thing for a virgin to look at. What possible pleasure could it afford you? None. No, no, you would not wish for that . . . Listen to me a moment. I have an emerald, a great round emerald that Caesar's favorite sent to me. Look into it and you can see things that are happening far away. Caesar himself wears an emerald like it when he goes to the circus. But mine is larger. It is the largest emerald in the world. Surely that is what you would like to have? Ask me for it an I will give it to you.

Salome, you know those white peacocks of mine, those marvelous white peacocks that walk about the garden between the myrtles and the tall cypresses. Their beaks are gilded, and the grains they eat are gilded too, and their feet are stained with purple. When they cry out the rain comes, and when they spread their tails the moon appears in the sky. They move two by two among the cypresses and the black myrtles and each has

31

a slave to care for it. Sometimes they fly atop the trees and sometimes they couch in the grass and beside the pool. The world cannot show any birds so marvelous as these. No king in the world possesses such birds. I am sure that even Caesar has no birds so beautiful. Well, then, I will give you fifty of my peacocks. They will follow you everywhere, and in the midst of them you will be like the moon surrounded by a great white cloud . . . I will give you all of them. Only, you must release me from my oath and not ask me for what you have asked.

The Dutchess Of Padua. 1883. Act III.

Guido decides not to take his revenge on the Duke, due to his love for Beatrice, the Duke's wife. He instead plans to leave a note, stating that he intended to kill the Duke, but spared him.

GUIDO

Now I am assured you know naught at all of love. Love is life's sacrament; it hath magic to charm virtue out of naught, and purifies from all the nauseous refuse of this world. It is the fire that refines the gold from dross, the van that sifts chaff and wheat, the Spring that from the hard-frozen soil lets innocency put forth her rosebuds. God walks no more amongst mankind - his image, Love, goes in His stead. The man who loves a woman knoweth the secret as well of the Creator as of the world created. There is no house so lowly, so poor and pityful, that, if the indwellers be pure of heart, Love shuns the same; but an if bloody murder knock at the Palace gate, and find an entrance, then creeps love forth and dies. That is the penalty ordained of God of sin. The bad man cannot love.

I take this to be woman's mission, - through the power of Love to save man's soul; love for my Beatrice hath taught me to see a more sublime, more holy vengeance, an if I spare the Duke, than in any bloody deed of murderous midnight violence, - young hands choking out an old man's life. Wasn't not for love's sake that Christ, who himself was Love incarnate, exhorted men to forgive their enemies?

The Dutchess Of Padua. 1883. Act III.

After deciding not to kill the Duke, Guido prays to God, explaining his actions, and giving further explanation regarding the letter that he plans to leave for the Duke, telling that he had spared his life.

GUIDO

Thou, father, knowest of my intent and art content with this nobler vengeance. Whenas I grant the man his life, I ween I am doing as thou would'st have done thyself. I cannot tell, father, whether human voice can break through the iron prison of the dead, whether the departed have any tidings of what we do and leave undone for their sakes. And yet, methinks, I feel a presence near me, like a shadow by my side, and meseems as though spirit kisses touched my lips and left them sanctified. *(He kneels.)* Oh father, canst thou not break the laws of Death and show thyself in bodily shape, that I may grasp thy hand? Nay, nay, 'tis naught. *(Rises.)* It is the midnight phantoms do befool us, the night deceives us like a puppet-showman, persuading us that what is not, is. 'Tis waxing late; I must now to my work. *(He pulls a letter from his bosom and reads.)* When he awakes and sees this letter and dagger beside it, disgust will take hold of him for his life. Will he mayhap repent and reform his ways? Or will he mock, because a young wight hath spared him, his bitter enemy? 'Tis all one to me. Thy errand, father, it is that I fulfil, - thy orders and my love's, which hath taught me to know thee as thou art.

The Duchess Of Padua. 1883. Act IV.

Guido is being held at the Hall of Justice after being accused of the Duke's murder by Beatrice. During his trial, he confesses to the deed in order to protect Beatrice.

GUIDO

(To the headsman.) Thou man of blood, turn not thine axe toward me before the time; who knows whether my death-hour be really come. Is mine the only neck among folk present here?To be brief: yesternight 'twas midnight when I scaled the Palace walls with a stout rope, bent on avenging my father's murderer; such as was my purpose, I do own it, Sir. Thus much will I confess, and this to boot: when cautiously I had climbed the steps that lead to the Duke's sleeping-room, and was stretching forth my hand to the scarlet curtain, that shook and shuddered in the storm, just then the white moon shone out in the sky and flooded the dark chamber with a silver sheen, the night light up its tapers for my service. Asleep lay the hated Duke, still cursing in his dreams, and at the thought of my father's slaying, - my father whom he bartered to the block, sold to the scaffold, I pierced the traitor's heart with this dagger here, which by mere chance I found there in the room.

The Ideal Husband. 1895. Act II.

*When Sir Robert Chiltern's secret of having sold shares in the
Suez Canal is revealed to his wife, Gertrude, she is unable to
forgive him, berates herself for having trusted him implicitly.
Here is his response:*

SIR ROBERT CHILTERN

There was your mistake. There was you error. The
error all women commit. Why can't you women love
us, faults and all? Why do you place us on monstrous
pedestals? We have all feet of clay, women as well as
men; but when we men love women, we love them
knowing their weaknesses, their follies, their
imperfections, love them all the more, it may be, for
that reason. It is not the perfect, but the imperfect, who
have need for love. It is when we are wounded by our
own hands, or by the hands of others, that love should
come to cure us - else what use is love at all? All sins,
except sin against itself, Love should forgive. All lives,
save loveless lives, true Love should pardon. A man's
love is like that. It is wider, larger, more human than a
woman's. Women think that they are making ideals of
men. What they are making of us are false idols
merely. You made your false idol of me, and I had not
the courage to come down, show you my wounds, tell
you my weaknesses. I was afraid that I might lose your
love, as I have lost it now. And so, last night you
ruined my life for me - yes, ruined it! What this
woman asked of me was nothing compared to what she
offered me. She offered me security, peace, stability.
The sin of my youth, that I had thought was buried,

36

rose up in front of me, hideous, horrible, with its hands at my throat. I could have killed it forever, sent it back into its tomb, destroyed its record, burned the witness against me. You prevented me. No one but you, you know it. And now what is there before me but public disgrace, ruin, terrible shame, the mockery of the world, a lonely dishonoured life, a lonely dishonoured death, it may be, some day? Let women make no more ideals of men! Let them not put them on altars and bow before them, or they may ruin other lives a completely as you - you whom I have so wildly loved - have ruined mine!

ORDER DIRECT

MONOLOGUES THEY HAVEN'T HEARD. *Karshner.*
Modern speeches written in the language of today.
MORE MONOLOGUES THEY HAVEN'T HEARD.
Karshner. More exciting living-language speeches.
SCENES THEY HAVEN'T SEEN. *Karshner.* Fresh,
contemporary scenes for men and women.
FOR WOMEN, MONOLOGUES THEY HAVEN'T HEARD.
Pomerance. Contemporary speeches for actresses.
MONOLOGUES FOR KIDS. *Roddy.* 28 wonderful speeches
for boys and girls. Modern, incisive.
MONLOUGUES FOR TEENAGERS. *Karshner.*
Contemporary speeches written in language that is *now.*
SCENES FOR TEENAGERS. *Karshner.* Scenes relevant to
today's teenage boys and girls.
DOWNHOME MONOLOGUES. *Karshner.* Speeches in the
language of rural America.
MONOLOGUES FROM THE CLASSICS. *ed. Karshner.* 35
speeches from Shakespeare, Marlowe & others.
SCENES FROM THE CLASSICS. *ed. Maag.* 18 famous
scenes from Shakespeare & others.
MONOLOGUES FROM RESTORATION PLAYS. *ed.*
Maag. A ready reference to great speeches from the period.
SHAKESPEARE'S MONOLOGUES HAVEN'T HEARD.
ed. Maag. Lesser known speeches from The Bard.
MONOLOGUES FROM CHEKHOV. *ed. Cartwright.*
Modern translations from Chekhov's major plays.
MONOLOGUES FROM BERNARD SHAW. *ed. Michaels.*
Great Speeches from the works of GBS.
MONOLOGUES FROM OSCAR WILDE. *ed. Michaels.* The
best of Wilde's urbane and dramatic wirting.

**All books $4.95. Enclose your check or money order (no
cash or C. O. D.) plus handling charges of $0.75 for the
first book, $0.25 for each additional book up to a
maximum of $1.50. California residents add 6%. Please
send orders to: DRAMALINE PUBLICATIONS, 10470
Riverside Drive, Suite #201, Toluca Lake, CA 91602.**